Animalographies

Beautiful Jim
The World's Smartest Horse

Jodie Parachini   illustrated by Dragan Kordić

Albert Whitman & Company
Chicago, Illinois

For educated horses everywhere—JP

To Ines—DK

Library of Congress Cataloging-in-Publication data is on file with the publisher.

Text copyright © 2021 by Jodie Parachini

Illustrations copyright © 2021 by Albert Whitman & Company

Illustrations by Dragan Kordić

First published in the United States of America in 2021 by Albert Whitman & Company

ISBN 978-0-8075-0611-0 (hardcover) • ISBN 978-0-8075-0612-7 (ebook)

Printed in China

10 9 8 7 6 5 4 3 2 1 WKT 26 25 24 23 22 21

Design by Aphelandra

For more information about Albert Whitman & Company, visit our website at www.albertwhitman.com.

Some horses are fast—like racing sensation Seabiscuit—
and some horses are famous for starring on TV and
in books—like Black Beauty—but this is the true story
about a horse that could read, write, and do math.
The smartest horse in the world…

Me!

I'm Beautiful Jim Key.

I'm a celebrity. I had my picture in all the major newspapers, and I was even a star attraction at the world's fair in 1904! But I'll start at the beginning…

I was born in 1889 in Tennessee. My mom, Lauretta, had been a circus horse, and my dad, Tennessee Volunteer, was a strong and healthy stallion. I was supposed to grow up to be a famous racehorse, but sometimes things don't work out as planned.

I was frail and weak as a colt, with a dingy, knotted coat, and it took me a long time to learn how to do things—even simple tasks, like standing upright.

MY DIARY ♘ **1889**

This skill called walking is tricky! Every time I put a hoof down, my leg crumples. Last time I tried, I made it three steps before wobbling and falling over. How embarrassing. I hate feeling like the ugly duckling. I really want to learn how to run and play like the other foals, but I just feel so teeter-tottery. I don't know if that's a real word—there's so much to learn as a colt.

My human had wanted to name me something graceful and majestic and biblical. But when he saw me stumble and stagger in the stables, he decided to name me after his neighbor, a man who wobbled when he walked. So that's how I became Jim. (The "Beautiful" part came later.)

My human was a man named William Key. Most people called him Doc. He wasn't a typical medical doctor. William was born into slavery in 1833 and grew up on a plantation in Shelbyville, Tennessee. As a child, William loved animals—at six years old he taught a rooster and a yellow dog to perform tricks, and he had a special fondness for ponies, mules, and horses.

Enslaved people were usually barred from learning to read and write, but William's master allowed William to join his white sons, Merit and Alexander, in their daily lessons.

William was an eager and perceptive student. He loved to read manuals about animal medicine, and he experimented with remedies to heal hurt or sick farm animals. Sometimes the townspeople even asked him to help human patients.

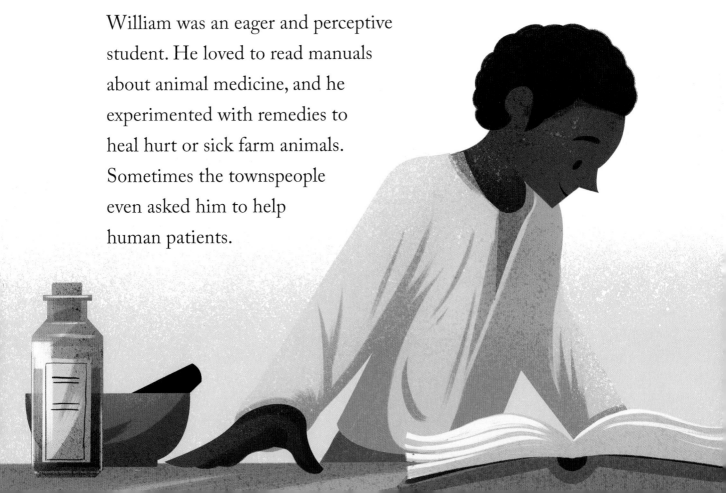

During the Civil War, from 1861 to 1865, William was tasked with many difficult roles, including working as a medic and surgeon for wounded soldiers and horses on the Confederate side (his master's sons were fighting for the South), a secret spy for the Union, and even a guide to help slaves reach the North. But when the war ended, William "Doc" Key, no longer enslaved, was free to follow his dream of working with animals.

As a self-taught veterinarian and medicine salesman in Tennessee, Doc became a wealthy man. His homemade medicine, called Keystone Liniment (made with a secret ingredient: calcium from the limestone rocks in his county), was said to heal all kinds of problems, from bruises and cuts to lameness and cholera.

I could tell immediately that Doc was a special owner and trainer. He was kind and gentle and really cared about us animals.

MY DIARY ♘ 1890

Doc let me sleep inside his house last night. It was cold in the yard, and I like it better next to the warm fire. Doc's wife, Lucinda, wasn't too happy about having a horse in the house, but she just shook her head and sighed. Today, she said, "Jim, would you like a piece of apple?" I nodded my head. Boy, was she surprised!

My human family started teaching me tricks like those they would teach a dog: rolling over, fetching sticks, and sitting up for treats. It was easy! So easy that I started teaching myself a few tricks too. Like how to unfasten the gate to the pasture and how to open the drawer the apples were stored in.

Doc must have known that I wanted to learn more, so he started teaching me the alphabet and how to count.

How does a horse spell words? Simple. I don't usually write them down—hooves aren't as expert as hands—so Doc had a set of letters made from cardboard and tin. We started with *A*. Doc would line the letter with sugar, and I would lick it clean while he said *A* over and over again. It took six months for me to understand the alphabet game, but by then, he didn't even need to paste the *A* with sugar— he would ask me to bring him the letter *A* card with my teeth, and he would reward me with a cube of sugar when I got it right. After that, the rest of the letters came more easily. Numbers too.

Doc was a great teacher. He never punished or whipped me if I did anything wrong. He said that patience and kindness were the only two skills needed when working with animals. Oh, and treats. I LOVE apples and sugar cubes.

Over the next few years, Doc taught me to recognize colors, flags, coins, and playing cards, too, but we focused mostly on putting letters together to form words. Doc would say the word *cat*, and I would use my mouth to grab the letter cards *C*, *A*, and *T* in the correct order and slide them onto slots in a special rack he made for me. Sometimes, Doc would put chalk in my mouth, and I would write my name, but chalk tastes awful, so I wasn't very good at writing.

Doc and I were starting to attract attention, so after seven years, Doc said it was time to hit the road.

MY DIARY ♘ JUNE 1, 1897

Today, Doc Key brought me to the Tennessee Centennial Exposition, a great big fair. I was nervous performing for such a large crowd, especially when I saw the president of the United States, William McKinley, sitting in the front row. Doc asked me to pick out the president's name from a list of cards on my rack. I brought the MCKINLEY card to Mr. McKinley and bowed. He called me "astonishing and entertaining." Thank you, Mr. President!

The news reporters in Tennessee were astounded too.
They called me "Beautiful" in their reviews, so Doc added it
to my name. Beautiful Jim Key. I like the way that sounds!

MCKINLEY

The Tennessee fair was where Doc met animal-lover and manager Albert R. Rogers who knew that I could be a star. Mr. Rogers became our partner and set up a tour of theaters and music halls across the country.

Beautiful Jim
NEW ORLEANS
1901

BOSTON MECHANICS FAIR
1903
JIM KEY

THE MOST WONDERFUL EDUCATED HORSE IN THE WORLD
PERFORMING ASTOUNDING FEATS OF INTELLIGENCE THAT DELIGHT AND AMAZE
CHICAGO
1902
Jim.
BEAUTIFUL
JIM KEY

He Re
Co

JIM KE

NATIONAL EXPORT EXPOSITION
Philadelphia Sept to Nov 1900

DERFUL
KEY

TIMORE
1899

JIM K
Come See the
Wonderful
in the Wo

My show was becoming a big hit.
I performed a variety of skills:

- ♘ moving the hands on a clock to tell the correct time

- ♘ using a telephone

- ♘ sorting the mail into the proper slots at a "post office"

- ♘ "fainting" when Doc joked that he was going to sell me

- ♘ putting money in a cash register and giving the correct change using my teeth

- ♘ playing a hand organ

- ♘ spelling out the book, chapter, and verse when Doc would recite Bible passages (I only know ones that mention horses)

- ♘ solving arithmetic problems using numbers up to thirty (I once answered an audience-member's question: "What's seven times three plus nine divided by three minus seven?" I tapped my hoof on the ground three times as my answer. I was right!)

Doc and I even starred in our own play on Broadway in New York. I loved seeing my name in lights! It was called *The Scholar and the Model Office Boy*. I played both parts in the title. In the first act, Doc played a professor who was teaching me to read, and in the second act, I pretended I had a job and did all sorts of office work. We got a standing ovation!

MY DIARY ♘ ST. LOUIS, 1904

I'm at the world's fair! I thought performing on Broadway was exciting, but this place is amazing. There are wonderful inventions everywhere I look: the very first T-shirts and baby incubators, Wilhelm Roentgen's mysterious "X-ray machine," and even strange waffles from Italy, called ice-cream cones. But people are coming from far and wide to see me (and they're even paying fifteen cents for my show. That's a LOT of money.)

My fans were growing more famous by the day. Educator
Booker T. Washington came to see me. So did President
Theodore Roosevelt's daughter, Alice, bandleader John
Philip Sousa, and the future president, William H. Taft.

Doc and Mr. Rogers thought that all this fame could really help the world understand that animals should be treated nicely. In the early 1900s, many humans considered horses as beasts fit only to pull a cart or carriage. But some people started to wonder whether animals could think or feel pain. New organizations such as the American Humane Association and Humane Education Society were taking shape and looking for spokespeople—or in my case, a spokeshorse!

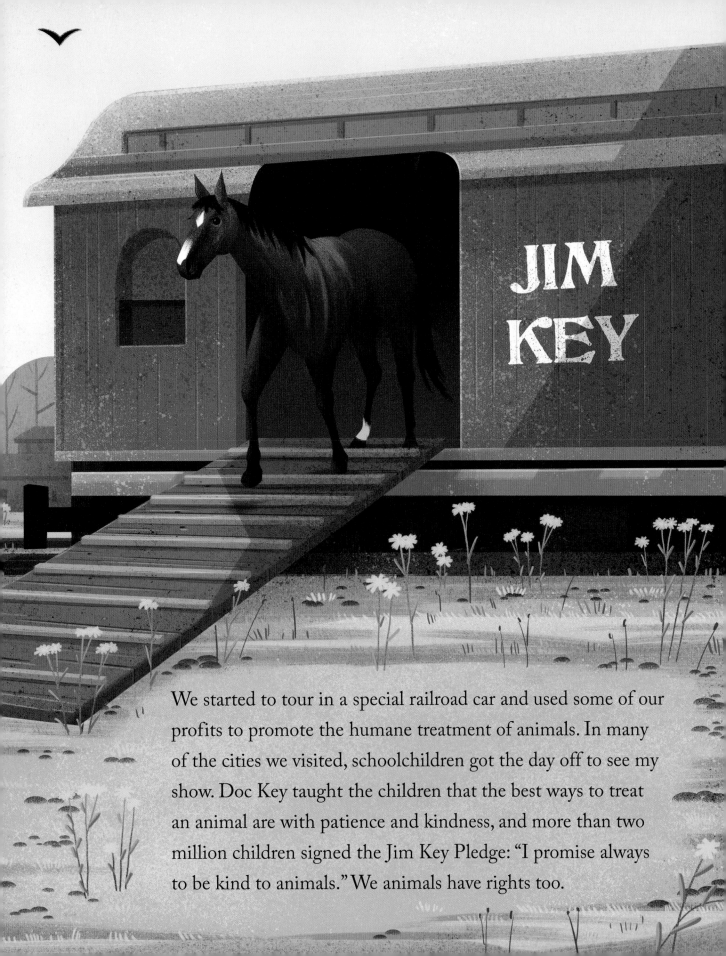

We started to tour in a special railroad car and used some of our profits to promote the humane treatment of animals. In many of the cities we visited, schoolchildren got the day off to see my show. Doc Key taught the children that the best ways to treat an animal are with patience and kindness, and more than two million children signed the Jim Key Pledge: "I promise always to be kind to animals." We animals have rights too.

In 1906 the *Minneapolis Journal* called me the "highest priced, most educated, and most talked about horse in the world." Finally, after nine years of touring, I was ready for a rest, so Doc and I headed back to Shelbyville to live out the remainder of our days in peace and solitude. Oh, and for me to eat as many apples as possible.

MY DIARY  1912

Some people said that my act was a hoax—that Doc was somehow giving me the answers the whole time. But I just tell them that scientists from Harvard—that big university in Massachusetts—came and examined the show. And they could find no example of any tomfoolery; instead, they credited it to pure animal intelligence.

Animal intelligence. That means I was really, really smart. And kindness, not cruelty, helped me get there.

Fact Sheet

BEAUTIFUL JIM KEY

1889–1912 (23 years old)

species: *Equus caballus*

breed: Arabian-Hambletonian mix

color: mahogany bay (a deep brown), with white patches down my nose and on two feet (like stockings), plus a little white mark on my forehead

hair: curly black mane and long black tail (almost to the ground)

height: 16 hands high (A hand is an ancient way to measure horses. One hand equals 4 inches, so I was about 5 feet, 3 inches from the ground to the top of my shoulders.)

best friend: Besides Doc, my best friend and traveling companion was Monk (a scruffy black-and-white dog who liked to stand on my back for pictures).

nicknames: the Equine King (*equine* means horse), Marvel of the Twentieth Century

favorite trick: The nation's favorite was when I stuck my entire head in a glass barrel full of water to retrieve a silver dollar from the bottom without drinking a drop of the water.

other amazing achievements: Humane groups across America set up spelling bees with fourth-, fifth-, and sixth-graders to see if they could win against a horse. I had to spell words such as *constitution* and *physics*. I nearly always won.

DOC KEY, SLAVERY, AND THE CIVIL WAR

The Civil War was fought from 1861–1865 between the Northern states that were against slavery and the Southern states that wanted to keep slaves. Doc Key lived in Tennessee, a Southern state that used slaves as its main workforce. Black people were taken against their will from Africa and other countries and forced to work on plantations and farms. In most areas of the South, it was illegal to teach people who were enslaved to read or write, which makes Doc's story unusual. And the amount of independence he was given to care for horses and people across the county was even more unusual.

When the war ended, four million enslaved Americans, including Doc Key, were freed. Rather than move North to states that had been against slavery, as many former slaves did, Doc stayed close to his former master's home and even used his own earnings to pay off his master's debts and send Merit and Alexander to Harvard. Grateful to have been given an education, Doc continued to share his love of learning with those around him, especially with one lucky recipient—Beautiful Jim Key.